LITTLE THOUGHTS ABOUT A
BIG GOD

Practical Life Lessons for Exceptional Living

BY ROB JAMES

Unless otherwise stated, all scriptures are taken from the NEW CENTURY VERSION (NCV)®. Copyright © 2005 by Thomas Nelson, Inc. Used by permission. All rights reserved.

Scripture quotations marked MSG are taken from The Message. Copyright © 1993, 1994, 1995, 1996, 2000, 2001, 2002. Used by permission of NavPress Publishing Group.

Scripture quotations marked NLT are taken from the Holy Bible, New Living Translation, copyright © 1996, 2004, 2007 by Tyndale House Foundation. Used by permission of Tyndale House Publishers, Inc., Carol Stream, Illinois 60188. All rights reserved.

Scripture quotations marked ESV are from The Holy Bible, English Standard Version® (ESV®), copyright © 2001 by Crossway, a publishing ministry of Good News Publishers. Used by permission. All rights reserved.

ISBN: 978-1-9997292-6-4

Copyright © 2018 Rob James
All rights reserved.
Published by Generous Heart.

FOREWORD

Rob has been producing weekly thoughts for various local newspapers and radio stations for more than thirty years, thoughts that have resonated with people of all ages, whatever their background or religious persuasion. This 'little' book contains a selection of these and will hopefully prove a helpful reminder that God is bigger than anything we are facing today or might even face tomorrow.

When the struggles of life come, our number one focus must be to rely on truth. Truth can be difficult to uncover in this world, but God's promises are secure. To remember that God is more significant than anything should be first and foremost in our thoughts. To praise Him for WHO HE IS should be our heart's desire.

God is more significant than anything and will encourage your heart and soul! Read the stories, meditate on them. He wants a relationship with you, and He wants to demonstrate that He really does love you.

Philip Bishop
Author, and co-founder of Generous Heart
(Generousheart.co.uk and Growmytrueself.org)

INTRODUCTION

As finite creatures, we can never adequately describe or explain our infinite God, but we can be wonderfully blessed when we seek to discover His truths and ways. And the Bible clearly shows us that such a search is never in vain:

"You will search for me. And when you search for me with all your heart, you will find me! I will let you find me," says the Lord. (Jeremiah 29:13-14).

Jesus Himself said something similar:

"Ask, and God will give to you. Search, and you will find. Knock, and the door will open for you. Yes, everyone who asks will receive. Everyone who searches will find. And everyone who knocks will have the door opened." (Matthew 7:7-8).

This book is a small collection of some of my thoughts about God's goodness and greatness. It is an attempt to communicate the wonderful nature of the God who can speak to us through very ordinary and everyday circumstances. These thoughts have helped me to grasp a little bit more of who He is, and I trust that they will communicate something of the depths of His love and the beauty of His splendour to you, too.

I have shared with you 52 thoughts, which will allow you to reflect on one thought per week, and they are divided into sections according to the themes contained within them. However, you can read this book in whichever way suits you best. I simply pray that you will spend some time thinking about our great creator and how you should respond to Him so that He might bless you in ways that surprise and delight you.

Rob James

Pastor, author, and co-founder of Generous Hearts (generousheart.co.uk)

THE WONDERFUL WORKS OF GOD

"And these are only a small part of God's works. We only hear a small whisper of him. Who could understand God's thundering power?"

Job 26:14.

1

Special Effects

I can't even begin to imagine what it must be like to be a refugee, but I do know what God can do in the lives of those who feel abandoned and abused. Lorraine (not her real name) was so badly treated that she ended up as a drug-addicted prostitute at the tender age of seventeen. She had no home other than a tent in the local woods, and her future was extremely bleak. Indeed, she had a dream in which she saw her own dead body, and it scared her enough to start looking for help. Her GP advised her that the only place he knew could help her at the time was run by a group of Christians, but Lorraine refused because she did not want to get involved with a group of 'Bible bashers'. Finally, though, in sheer desperation, she accepted his advice and that decision saved her life. Much to her relief, she discovered that no one wanted to 'push religion down her throat', they simply wanted to care for her. And they did so, lovingly and patiently. And then, one day, a member of staff said something that transformed her life forever. "Lorraine," she said, "you are very special." Lorraine is a Christian now and living a deeply fulfilling, healthy life. And it all happened because of five simple words! It's worth remembering every time we're with someone else, for like us, they too have been created in the image of God.

2

Clean Hands Open Minds

was intrigued to read that Dr Gina Radford, Deputy Chief Medical Officer, suggested that our failure to wash our hands with soap for a minimum of 45 seconds (about as long as it takes to sing the first verse of *God save the Queen*) is leading to infections, and thereby contributing to the problem of antibiotic resistance.

And I couldn't help smiling when I read her comments, too, because if she had been living in the 1840s, she would have been ridiculed and reviled in a way we would find difficult to comprehend today. For that was what happened to Ignaz Semmelweis when he tried to show his medical colleagues that fewer patients died when doctors and nurses washed their hands.

So why were they so resistant to his arguments? I think one writer summed it up nicely when he wrote: "Prejudices and jealousies blinded his colleagues to the truth." Sadly, prejudice can prove just as potent when it comes to trusting God, for I frequently find people 'switching off' when I try to tell them what He can do for them. But like hand washing, the evidence is there for all to see.

He can transform lives in the most amazing ways. Only this week, for example, I spent some time with a church leader who came to faith when he was a heroin addict and serving a prison sentence. He was given a Bible, and the rest, as he would say, is history. God gave him something better than clean hands; He gave him a clean heart. And if He can do that for him, I know He can do it for anybody.

3

JESUS NEXT DOOR

I've never visited Israel, although it's not for want of trying. I first planned a trip there when I was at university and won a scholarship to travel around the Eastern Mediterranean. But yet another outbreak of conflict put an end to that particular project. And it's been like it ever since. Each plan has come unstuck, and as much as I would love to wander around the streets of ancient Jerusalem or visit the ancient fortification Masada, I'm going to have to wait and see if my dream will ever be realised.

But as I have been reflecting, I have been reminding myself that I don't have to go to Bethlehem to find Jesus, because I regularly encounter Him in the faces of the needy. For this is what He taught His disciples:

"Then the King will say to those on his right, 'Enter, you who are blessed by my Father! Take what's coming to you in this kingdom. It's been ready for you since the world's foundation. And here's why:

I was hungry and you fed me,
I was thirsty and you gave me a drink,
I was homeless and you gave me a room,
I was shivering and you gave me clothes,
I was sick and you stopped to visit,
I was in prison and you came to me.'"
(Matthew 25:34-36, MSG).

Put simply, I don't have to travel to Israel to have a close encounter with God. He could be waiting for me next door.

LOVE IS PATIENT

Lewis Misselbrook had the most incredible smile and the most loving of hearts. He also had the most engaging way of sharing the Christian message, because it was shaped by the conviction that God loves us all unconditionally and expects us to copy His behaviour.

Lewis understood God's love is patient, and he illustrated this well in his superb little book, *Love Won Another*. He tells the story of a young girl named Laura and her caring psychiatrist, Richard D'Ambrosio. Laura had suffered terribly as a young child and, as a result, she had withdrawn into her own private world. But D'Ambrosio was determined to reach her no matter how long it took, and in a determined effort to achieve this, he purchased a doll's house construction kit. And so, twice a week, when Laura came into his office, he gently but steadily built the house. Two years later, she had still not responded in any way, and so he went out and bought kits to build both the furniture and the people to live in the house. And he carried on constructing until sometime later, to his utter delight, she reached out a hand and moved a chair.

Now that was but the beginning of the healing process. In fact, it took another four years before Laura was well enough to be discharged from D'Ambrosio's care as a perfectly normal, happy girl. But it was worth it, and as I read that moving story, I found myself echoing Lewis' heartfelt prayer that we might be able to love people with God's kind of infinitely patient love.

5

NOWT SO QUEER AS FOLK

I've often heard it said that there's "nowt so queer as folk". I couldn't help thinking that when I was pondering the familiar story of the Wise Men again the other day.

I've read it many times before, of course, but I was particularly struck this time by the reaction of the religious leaders Herod called in to advise him on the birthplace of the future Messiah. If anyone 'knew their stuff', they did, and like every other devout Jew of the day, they were longing for their long-awaited King to come. For when He did, it would mean an end to foreign oppression. As far as they were concerned, everything would be 'hunky dory' when He turned up. And yet, they chose to do nothing. Herod took the Wise Men seriously enough to organise a massacre, but his leaders just listened and went back to their daily routine as if nothing significant had happened at all.

I'm not sure why they behaved like this, but I do know they missed out badly, unlike the shepherds and the Wise Men who did a bit of investigating to see if the things they were being told were really true.

Lots of people behave in exactly the same way today. They sing carols, watch nativity plays and hear about the God who loves us so much that He was willing to go to any lengths to prove it. But it all ends there. And that makes me sad because the child who was born in Bethlehem offers us something no one else can. How daft can you be? It's worth checking out – surely?

THE WISDOM OF GOD

*Our Lord is great and very powerful.
There is no limit to what he knows.*

Psalm 147:5.

6

GIVING WHAT WE CAN

I guess most of us have been in situations that seem to stretch our faith to the limit. Challenges can come in all sorts of guises, but for my friend, Stevo, his moment came in the early 1990s when a flood forced refugees into his city.

Stevo was the pastor of a small Baptist church in the Croatian city of Rijeka at the time, and many of those desperate refugees had fled from the devastated town of Vukovar. They were traumatised, shell-shocked and in great material need. And I can still remember the day when Stevo told me how, faced with this monumental challenge, he opened a kitchen cupboard and saw a can of beans. Now, he could have been overwhelmed by the size of the task, but he concluded that if he only had one tin of beans, he could at least give that. And so, he did. Then, to his utter amazement, God sent him cans and cans of beans, and he was able to distribute massive amounts of humanitarian aid through a Christian agency that came to be known as 'My Neighbour'.

I will always be grateful to Stevo for reminding me that when we want to help others, the greatest obstacle is our willingness to give what we already have. For if we are willing to give that, then we will quickly find God is more than able to supply the rest.

7

SIGNIFICANTLY INSIGNIFICANT

I guess I will never know his name, but we owe him a great deal even if he's never realised it. I thought of him again when I heard that Fidel Castro had finally died at the grand old age of 90.

Let me explain. I am old enough to remember the Cuban missile crisis of 1962, a moment when it can be confidently said we came closer to thermonuclear war than at any other time in human history.

It was Robert Kennedy's biographer who alerted me to his importance. It would seem that at the height of the confrontation, Kennedy wanted to warn the Soviet authorities that they were playing with fire because (and I quote), "he didn't know how much longer his brother could control the hawks and the military." This prompted the Soviet ambassador, Alexander Dobrynin, to write an account of his meeting and send it to Moscow as quickly as he could. But incredibly, he had to do it by Western Union courier because there were no other means of immediate transmission at the time!

Is it any wonder then that Ambassador Dobrynin prayed that this young man would not stop off for a Coke or waste time dallying with his girlfriend?

Stories like this remind us that we should be thankful for those who carry out their duties faithfully. We owe them a lot, perhaps more than the appreciation they received at the time. And maybe it's worth reminding ourselves that we may never know the importance of something we've been asked to do. We can learn a lot from a young man and his bicycle.

8

STEPS OF FAITH

I love travelling and have seen some spectacular places in my time. Mount Fuji, Ephesus, the Alamo, they're all logged in the memory bank, and I would go back to any or all of them tomorrow, given half a chance.

But for sheer wonder, the Grand Canyon has to come first. It's not just its beauty; it's so big, it simply takes your breath away. Indeed, I can think of nothing more awesome than to stand on the edge of the north rim and gaze into the abyss, which I've been told is a mile deep.

Much as I would like to re-visit the canyon, I don't know if I'll ever be brave enough to venture out onto the Skywalk (an amazing horseshoe-shaped cantilever bridge with a glass floor). The deck may be capable of withstanding a 100-pound load per square foot along with wind and seismic forces that constantly batter it, but I still find the thought of stepping out onto 'nothing' more than a little unnerving!

When I stop and think about it, I suppose I should find it easier than many because of what I've seen God do in my life. I've never seen Him, but I know that whenever I've stepped out in faith, He has proved completely dependable. So, who knows? Perhaps I'll have a go at that Skywalk one day after all.

9

HALF TRUTHS

Strange as it might seem, I reckon it's possible to be absolutely right and completely wrong at one and the same time. Take the group of Sicilian monks I read about recently. It would seem that they spent their days making, then unmaking and then re-making wicker baskets. They believed the world had a limited shelf life and, because of that, felt there was no need to do anything to change it.

Their first assumption was correct, of course. This world, indeed this universe, will not last forever. Jesus told us that, and He should know, given the fact that He came back from the dead! He has promised to return to earth one day, and when He does, He will restore everything to its pristine glory. One of His closest friends heard and penned these words from heaven: *"He will wipe every tear from their eyes, and there will be no more death or sorrow or crying or pain."* (Revelation 21:4, NLT). All these things will disappear – forever.

But when it comes to their behaviour, those Sicilian monks were as misguided as the man (or was it a woman?) who suggested the moon is made of cheese. Far from putting our feet up and taking things easy, God has told us that we are to do everything we can to make this world a better place to live in. And we don't have to devise earth-shattering plans to do it, because Jesus has assured us that even a cup of cold water given in His name would not go unnoticed – and not just by the recipient, either!

10

PREDICTABLY UNPREDICTABLE

I love listening to peoples' stories, especially when they're sharing their experiences of God. The God I have come to know and love is so 'predictably unpredictable'. I can never put Him in a box, and He constantly does things that go way beyond my expectations.

Take my new friend Mark. I met Mark when I was working for a church in Tenerife. A decade or so ago, Mark was but one of many who would say, "I don't do God." But everything changed when a gas explosion left him so badly injured that his doctors told him he would never walk again. I can't even begin to imagine how he must have felt. A word like 'depressed' seems far too trite.

But then, to his utter amazement, Jesus appeared to him in a vision, offering him a new life (the medics said he was hallucinating). It was a very long haul, and it took an enormous amount of determined effort, but Mark did learn to walk again, even though his doctors had constantly told him that he was living in denial. In fact, we played paddle tennis together.

I know other people who have not been healed so miraculously, and I have no explanation to why that is so, but I have seen enough to know that God is capable of doing the impossible, and He constantly does. Whatever the outcome, however, He wants to assure us that He always has our best interests at heart.

11

A LASTING MEMORY

We've never met, but she has clearly read something I've written about the man who changed her life. In fact, she would go so far as to use the word 'saved'. And if what she has told me is true, her life was certainly in a mess until she had a life-changing encounter with her hero. Strangely enough, though, she never met him, because he died some fifteen years before she'd even heard of him. But once she had, she told me, he became an inspiration.

And she's not alone in this, because I know of at least one highly successful CEO who has been inspired by the story of William Marshal, 'The Greatest Knight', and he died in May 1219, some 750 years before this particular CEO was born!

We often forget that our lives can have a lasting impact on others, and it can prove far more influential than we think. Unkind words and thoughtless comments, for example, can prove terribly destructive. I know that's true because I was once told that I was useless at woodwork and, as a result, for me, DIY has always been LITO (leave it to others!).

Thankfully, we can also have the opposite effect and leave a legacy that will encourage others to reach their God-given potential. After all, that is how Jesus behaved.

And so, as I enter each new day, I will do my best to promote 'freedom of speech' and 'freedom of religion', but hopefully, in such a compassionate and generous way that I will attract more and more people to the One who is rightly called 'The Way, the Truth and the Life' (see John 14:6). I think I could rest easy if I thought I would be remembered that way.

UNDERSTANDING GOD

"God's voice thunders in wonderful ways; he does great things we cannot understand."

Job 37:5.

12

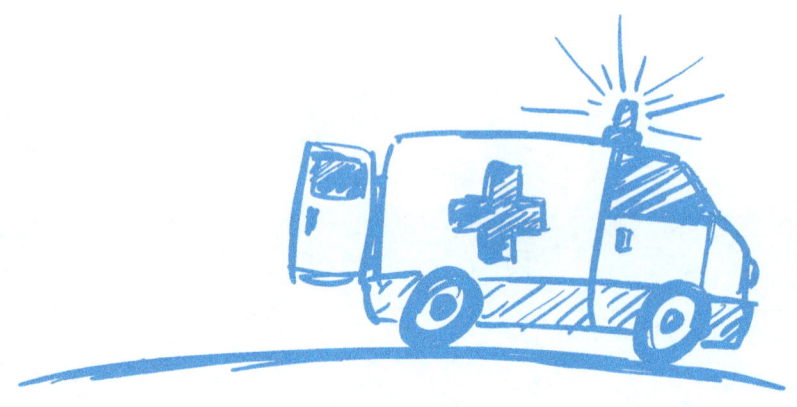

ALMOST SPEECHLESS

I would be the first to acknowledge that we live in an increasingly secular society. The number of people who don't 'do God' is growing rapidly. And I can readily identify with them, because there was a time when I didn't 'do God', either. In fact, I did all I could not to! But much to everyone's surprise, I had a complete change of heart and became a sold-out believer. Even more amazingly, I became a pastor.

I vividly remember one well-known editor telling me that, as far as he was concerned, God simply didn't exist and, as a result, I found it very difficult to mention the 'G-word' in any copy I produced for him. That is, until the day I told him how I came to drive an ambulance across Europe.

It took place in the mid-1990s when the former Yugoslavia was being torn apart by a bitter civil war. I was a member of a team taking aid to groups of refugees with whom we were in contact. We received an urgent call asking if we could supply them with an ambulance, which seemed a pretty ludicrous request at the time. But we did what we always did: we prayed. And to our amazement, about an hour or two later, we received a telephone call from a health authority asking us if we needed any ambulances because they had four that they no longer required. My editor friend simply gasped and said, "Good God!" To which I responded, "You've got it in one."

13

SWEET TALK

Dick Beesely was a great guy and nothing if not an encourager. And he was incredibly kind, too. Put quite simply, he was possessed of a very generous spirit. I realised that very early on in our friendship when we were chatting at the end of a Sunday morning church service. I was trying to explain why I had taken a particular course of action, and as can sometimes happen, I was getting a little tongue-tied in the process. But as I struggled to make sense of what I was trying to say, he simply smiled and said, "Let me tell you a story." And he went on to say something I have never, ever forgotten. It seems that a few years before this while travelling through the United States, he and his wife, Audrey, had stopped off for a coffee. As he was drinking, he noticed something written on the sugar packet the waitress had placed in his saucer. It read: "You don't have to explain to your friends, and your enemies will never believe you anyway."

Dick's little tale stopped me dead in my tracks because he was obviously trying to tell me that he trusted me. That little observation has been a constant reminder to me that I can always trust my friends, even when we disagree. It has also challenged me to check out the way I react when I don't understand something a friend has said or done. For I know it is all too easy to let prejudice determine my opinion. Above all, though, Dick's little story has been a constant reassurance that in the last analysis, I don't have to explain anything to God. For my heavenly dad knows me 'warts and all' and still wants to be my best friend.

14

USING OUR LITTLE GREY CELLS

None of us are perfect. We all make mistakes. I can readily recall the embarrassment I felt, for example, when I turned up for a meeting a month early! Having said that, I do take comfort from the fact that I knew a head teacher who sent one of his staff members on a training course a whole year later than he should have! But I reckon Laura McKenzie must be a contender for the Guinness Book of Records when it comes to messing things up.

I came across Laura's story a little while ago. It seems that she stopped her car at a red light somewhere in the Australian outback, and being a very law-abiding lady, she was determined not to move until it changed to green. And that's where it all went wrong because the light didn't change; it stayed on red. Laura was finally found two days later, completely dehydrated and slumped across the steering wheel. She had an explanation, of course. And so, when she was pulled from her car, she told her rescuers that she wasn't aware the lights were broken.

People make big mistakes when it comes to Jesus, too. Some think He's a sort of fictional fairy-tale character who never really existed. Others operate on the understanding that He is irrelevant and, as a result, they are not interested in Him. I suppose it only goes to show how mistaken we can be about some things.

15

COMPLETELY SOLD OUT

Taking a funeral is never easy. I'm always conscious of the raw emotions that can be present as well as the potential for saying – or not saying – the right thing. But I do count it a great privilege to be given the opportunity to show a little bit of God's love at a time of great need. In addition, funerals provide us with a wonderful opportunity to celebrate the gift of life and the ways in which the deceased person has impacted the lives of those they knew.

I conducted the funeral service of my friend Lloyd. He was considered something of a 'country legend' in South West Wales and someone who proved to be a source of huge encouragement to me in my own broadcasting adventures.

I thought I knew a lot about Lloyd but, as so often happens, I discovered that what I knew was just the tip of the iceberg. And in so doing, I realised that Lloyd has much to teach us about the importance of commitment.

Lloyd was totally committed to presenting his weekly country show, something he did faithfully for nearly forty years. But little did I know, until I prepared his eulogy, that there was a time when he discovered that he would not be able to drive to work because of a severe snowstorm. Many of us would have called in and apologised for not being able to make it, but not Lloyd. He put his music in a rucksack and walked ten miles to catch a train.

Lloyd's attitude has had a profound effect on me personally, but his example has proved more than challenging; it has become a helpful reminder of God's commitment to us, too. For if we put our trust in Him, He will never let us down. As someone rightly said, "He will never leave us, not never, not no how."

16

A SERVANT HEART

never cease to be amazed by some of the things we read in the gospels. The disciples were just ordinary men and yet they came up with some of the most profound sayings imaginable.

Take the apostle John. A simple fisherman, he knew that every one of us is made in the image of God and are able to say and do things that reflect His character, whether we are Christians or not.

I was reminded of this when I went into a public washroom in Malaysia. As I turned around after washing my hands, I found myself facing the cleaner who was standing there with a smile on his face and a towel in his outstretched hands. I was amazed. He had no need to do that. But he was clearly eager to be of service. And I found myself thinking of Jesus and the way He behaved. He came to serve, not to be served, and in so doing, He showed us how we should live, too. I have no idea if that young man was a Christian, but of one thing I am sure: I saw something of Jesus in his behaviour that day, and it made me wonder how much of His servant nature is seen in me.

17

INSPIRATION

Jesus' early followers claimed He was unique. In fact, the more time they spent with Him, the more convinced they became that He was unlike any other man they had ever met. But why, and what did they think that meant? Perhaps the story that's told of nineteenth-century artist Paul Doré will help us understand that question a little better.

Doré was travelling across Europe but had forgotten his passport and, not surprisingly, the border guard refused to let him cross. At first, Doré was nonplussed, but then he had a bright idea. He picked up a pencil and started to draw. When the guard saw how well he could sketch, he smiled and waved him on. He reckoned that if he could draw like that, it simply had to be Doré!

A lot of people find it hard to believe that Jesus was God in the flesh. And I can understand why. How could, indeed why would, the creator of the universe become an ordinary human being? It can sound pretty far-fetched when you put it like that.

But I came to the conclusion long ago that anyone who can turn water into wine, feed 5,000 people when all He had to give them was the equivalent of a packed lunch, and rise from the dead must be in a category of His own.

One of His very closest friends put it this way: *"In the beginning the Word already existed. The Word was with God, and the Word was God … So the Word became human and made his home among us. He was full of unfailing love and faithfulness … to all who believed him and accepted him, he gave the right to become children of God."* (see John 1).

If we stop and think about it for a moment, it's obvious that, given the things He said about Himself, Jesus had to be mad, bad or the one He claimed to be. And it's worth remembering that His closest friends, those who lived with him 24/7 for three whole years, concluded He was telling the truth. And they were so convinced He had come to life again that they were willing to die rather than deny it.

Given all this, I reckon we'd have to be a bit crazy not to check Him out. What do you think?

18

NO LOOKING BACK

I would never have associated the prophet Jeremiah with Bridgend, but I will from now on – and all because of a used car showroom. I was walking past the aforementioned showroom when I noticed a large banner that boldly declared, "We are looking to your future, not your past." Not a bad advert. It certainly caught my attention. But it did far more than that: it reminded me of something the prophet Jeremiah said more than two and half thousand years ago. Addressing a depressed people who were trying to come to terms with a long and difficult exile, he told them, "God wants you to know that if you put your trust in Him, you have a bright future ahead of you."

That's just as true for us today. God is not so much interested in our past failings as in the possibilities that lie ahead of us. He can and will forgive anyone anything, and then give them a brand-new start. We can learn from our past, of course, and so we should. But we can do more than learn from it, we can also let it prompt us to grasp our God-given destinies. For in so doing, we will discover life as it's meant to be.

19

THE GOD OF HOPE

Some decisions are not just important, they can even prove life-changing. I discovered this more than twenty years ago when I joined a group of friends who were keen to help refugees in what was then worn-torn Yugoslavia. My life and my ministry have never been the same since. I watched God do amazing things, and I met some of the most incredible Christians you could ever get to know, and they have proved nothing less than inspirational. It was a valuable reminder that you never know what will happen when you allow God to take you out of your comfort zone!

Take Dessa. I first met her when I arrived in Rijeka in the winter of 1992. Her life was in ruins. She and her husband were fortunate to be alive. They had suffered terribly before escaping from Bosnia, but in the process, they had decided to put their future in God's hands. And like many a new Christian, Dessa took His promises seriously. She was pregnant but was told the child she was bearing was dead. Not daunted, Dessa laid hands on her own stomach and prayed. And to everyone's delight, her baby girl was born very much alive. Now, I don't know what you would have called the child, but Dessa named her daughter *Nada*, which means 'hope'. And she's still very much alive and a constant reminder that when we put our trust in the living God, there is always hope no matter how dark things seem at the time.

20

NOT DEAD YET

UNDERSTANDING GOD

I came across a fascinating story the other day about an Australian man called Paul Miller. Paul began to feel a little bit puzzled when his friends kept running up to him and hugging him in the street … until he discovered the reason for their joy! It seems that they had read of his death in a local newspaper and were thrilled to discover that it was a mistake. And Paul discovered that they weren't joking when he read his death notice, which said: "Miller, Paul Leslie. Will be a much-missed father, grandfather and friend."

But then, much to his astonishment, he discovered that it was not the paper's fault. They had not got it wrong. His son had placed the notice so that he could get some time off work to go whelk fishing. The advert cost him $16.80, but he thought it well worth the investment because it persuaded his boss to allow him seven days of bereavement leave.

I suppose we can see the funny side of it now, although I reckon that was not Paul Miller's immediate reaction. I don't think I would be smiling if one of my kids did that to me. But this rather odd story reminds us of a very important truth. People have constantly written off the church, but they've always ended up with 'egg on their face'. And for one simple reason: God can do some pretty amazing things in graveyards. After all, He did raise Jesus to life again. So next time you read a gloomy article about the church, just stop and think about Paul Miller for a moment. It might help you keep in touch with reality and may encourage you to pray a little more expectantly.

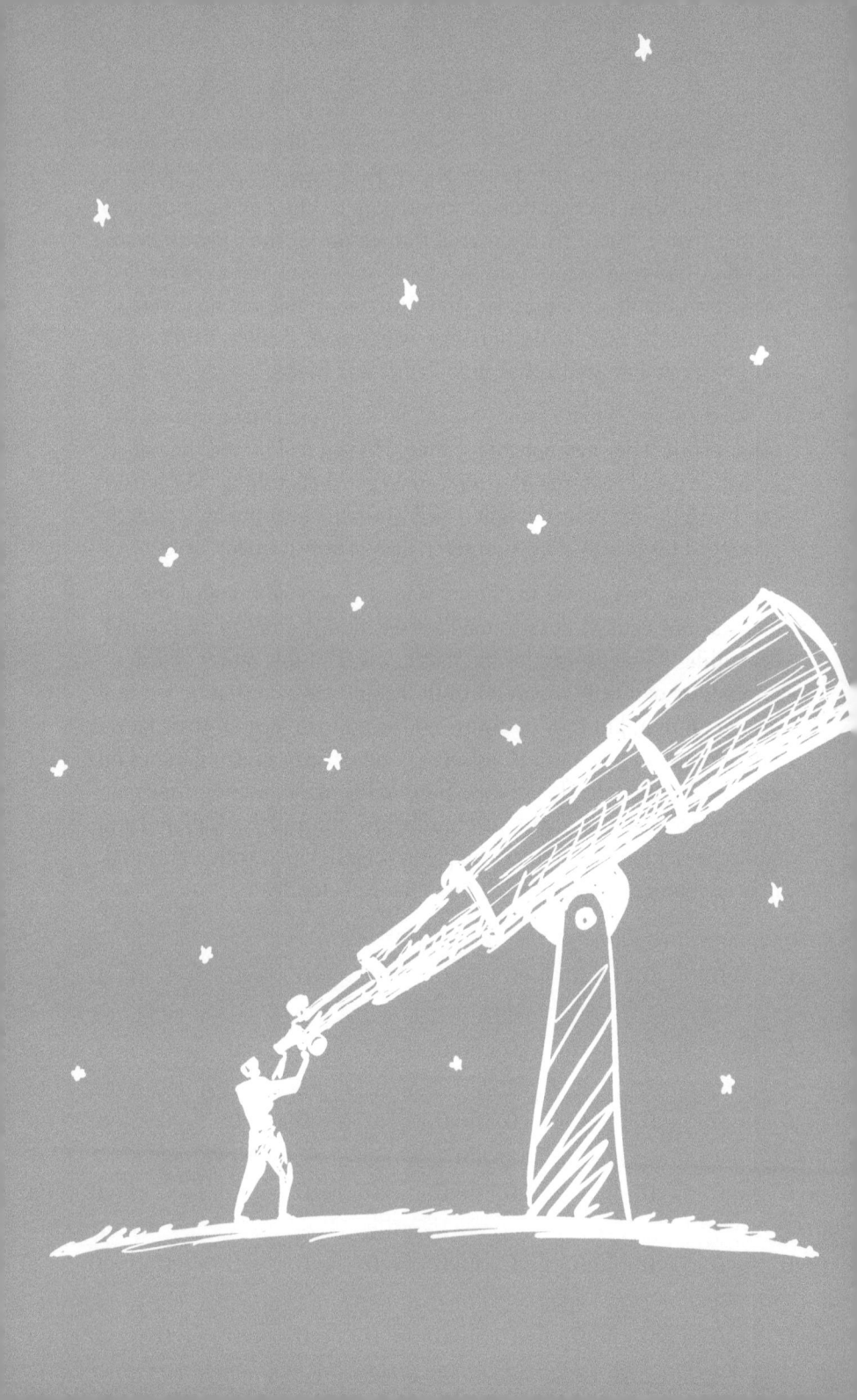

GOD EXHIBITED IN HIS WORKS OF CREATION AND PROVIDENCE

"*I am the Lord. There is no other God; I am the only God. I will make you strong, even though you don't know me, so that everyone will know there is no other God. From the east to the west they will know I alone am the Lord. I made the light and the darkness. I bring peace, and I cause troubles. I, the Lord, do all these things.*"

Isaiah 45:5-7.

21

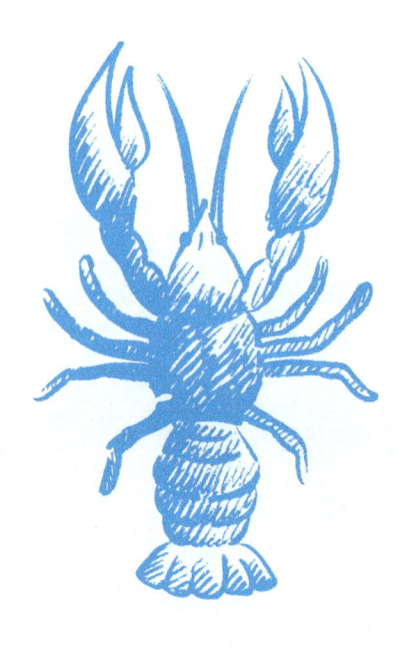

CHILDLIKE FAITH

I love Pembrokeshire, although I had no idea how lovely it was until I moved there in 1979. I grew up in Gwent and expected to serve God in South East Wales, but He had other plans. And I can truthfully say that my wife and I never cease to give thanks for the friendliness of Pembrokeshire's people and the spectacular beauty of its coastline.

Our grandchildren love it, too, none more than six-year-old Noah. Noah is a keen 'crabber' and takes every chance he can to wander around the rock pools to be found at Freshwater West, which is where he was one memorable Bank Holiday Saturday.

Noah was delighted because he discovered crab after crab. But it was the moment when he came across a dead crab that will stick long in my memory. "Bring it back to life, Noah," I suggested with a smile. But he was having none of that. As quick as a flash, he replied, "Don't be silly, only Jesus can do that!"

Now that's not bad for a six-year-old who has never been to theological college. And it's a timely reminder of what Jesus can do for us when we are faced with the challenges and pressures of everyday life. If He can conquer death, He is capable of doing anything.

22

NO NEED TO BECOME A MONK

I wasn't the most promising convert. In fact, I did everything I could to disprove the claims that were being made for Jesus. I even went so far as to give my girlfriend an ultimatum: choose me or choose God. Thankfully (if a little humbling at the time), she chose God.

And so, you can guess the sense of shock everyone felt when, a few years later, I concluded that God wanted me to sell our home, abandon my promising teaching career and train for the Baptist ministry. No one summed it up better than my mother, who despairingly told me one day that I "should have been a monk". She was deeply concerned because we had a young child (whom she idolised) and we were expecting another (as it turned out, we had one and got one free). Her concerns arose from the fact that we had no guaranteed source of income. We could only assure her that God would take care of our needs.

I found myself reflecting on this when attending a friend's funeral some time ago because he had baptised my mother many years later. I am sure she came to faith for all sorts of reasons, but I am convinced there was one reason in particular: God took care of all our needs throughout the three years I was in training, and He did so in the most amazing ways. He has done so ever since, too, which is why I can say with confidence that when we allow the Lord to be our shepherd, He will ensure we will never be in want.

23

A PIECE OF TOAST

I love taking school assemblies. Kids keep you on your toes and stretch your communication skills to the limit. But there are other rewards, too, such as the time I went into one of my local schools to say "Thank you" and to challenge the children to be kind. I had all the material I needed – a piece of toast. Now that may sound a little daft, but I can never forget that some twenty years ago a group of children from the same primary school discovered that I was part of a group that was seeking to help displaced Bosnian refugees and that we were trying to find a home for one family in particular.

And so, they immediately set about doing all they could to help us. They were not all that well off; in fact, their estate was one of the poorest in Wales. But that did not deter them. They were determined to help in any way, which, for some, meant going without one piece of toast in the breakfast club so that we could be given the money instead. And, as a result, they helped us purchase a new home for a family that had suffered terribly and lost everything in the process, a family I was happy to be reunited with recently.

And then it happened. I was introduced to a six-year-old boy who had been exceptionally kind that morning, so much so that we named him, "Mr Kindness". And as he looked at me with a disarmingly innocent smile, he whispered, "But kindness is my life." It got me thinking: "If only that were true of me." The world would be an infinitely better place if more of us could say that.

24

JESUS' ACCOUNT

It currently remains to be seen whether President Trump will EVER build 'that wall' on the Mexican border and who ends up paying for it! As we all know, it's much easier to make promises than to keep them.

I will never forget the first time I visited the Mexican border. I was there at the invitation of a small Baptist church that was located in the small town of Nogales. And I was amazed by what I saw. Even fifteen years ago, the number of people trying to enter the United States illegally was simply mind-boggling, as were the numbers of those succeeding despite the determined efforts of the armed guards placed there to stop them.

But my most enduring memory of that trip will always be that of the local 'lumber yard' where my Christian friends regularly went to buy timber. They were repairing a building that was being used to feed and clothe the hundreds of people who were turning up there every day. They had no financial resources of their own; they simply operated on the premise that they could trust God to meet their needs. And He was doing just that. In fact, even the local shopkeepers were becoming aware of it. Even so, you can imagine our surprise when we heard them tell a checkout assistant to put their bill on "the Jesus account".

We discovered later that the owners of the lumber yard had learned that, unlike many of us, God always pays His bills. And we shouldn't be surprised by that because Jesus told us that God's work done in God's way will never lack God's resources. And He can do that for one simple reason: He's not dead.

25

SPEECHLESS

GOD EXHIBITED IN HIS WORKS OF CREATION AND PROVIDENCE

The Prime Minister looked shell-shocked, and not surprisingly. A lot of people felt numb following what happened at Grenfell Tower in June 2017. Time alone will tell how a modern block of flats could become a towering inferno in such a short time (the Fire Brigade arrived within six minutes, but even this incredible response clearly proved futile).

And whoever would have thought that we would experience barbaric acts of terrorism comparable to those we have been able to observe from a safe distance over the years? How do we explain horrific acts like these in a supposedly civilised twenty-first-century democracy?

And then, of course, there's the raging anger. I understand the anger. As a pastor, I deal with bereaved people on a regular basis; I know only too well that it is a common, if often misunderstood, part of the grieving process.

It's for reasons like this we can be tempted to shy away from people who are coming to terms with their pain. We can feel very inadequate and think we simply wouldn't know how to handle their emotional turmoil. John (not his real name) has something to teach us here.

John learned a very valuable lesson when his son was killed in a road accident. "Prior to his death, I would never visit anyone who had lost a loved one," he told me. "I felt I would have nothing helpful to say."

But John's son's death had a revolutionary effect on his thinking because he discovered that the people who helped him most often had nothing to say. They simply came and sat, and often cried with him. "They didn't have to say anything," he explained, "and this experience has changed the way I think. From now on I am going to visit folk who have lost loved ones even when I feel completely useless. Through my loss, I've discovered how much it means to have friends who simply show they care."

26

REAPING WHAT YOU SOW

A friend shared this story with me, and I reckon it deserves a wider hearing. I hope it gets you thinking, too.

A lady was employed in a meat distribution factory. One day, as she was finishing work, she went into the 'cold room' to check something out. But to her dismay, the door closed behind her, and she found herself locked inside. She knocked and shouted as much as she could, but no one heard her desperate cries for help. Most of her fellow workers had already gone home, and even if they had still been there, they probably wouldn't have heard her anyway.

Thankfully, when she was close to unconsciousness, the door opened, and a very relieved security guard stepped in and helped her to safety.

The following day she asked her 'saviour' what had prompted him to look inside the 'cold room', given the fact that it was not part of his normal routine. This was his reply:

"I've been working in this factory for thirty-five years now, and hundreds of people come in and out every day. But you're one of the few who ever say "Hello" when you arrive and "Cheerio" when you're leaving work at night. Most tend to treat me as if I am invisible. You did the same when you clocked in this morning. I became suspicious when I noticed that I had not heard you say farewell as you normally do when you're on your way home. It made me think that I ought to take a look around to make sure you were OK."

And the moral of the tale? That's easy. It makes sense to have a positive impact on the people we meet because none of us knows what a day will bring.

27

DIVINE SMELLS

I have a beautiful wife, and she's a superb cook, too. I love opening the front door to be met by the smell of a freshly-cooked dinner or a newly-baked cake. There are few things in life to rival it – unless you're talking about the smell of fresh bread wafting up the stairs when you're battling to get out of bed on a Monday morning.

Have you ever realised that God loves certain smells, too? Well, the apostle Paul certainly thought so. We can see that from something he told some of his Christian friends living in the Roman colony of Philippi. Paul was alone and in prison. He was in great need and was facing the very real possibility of execution. His friends were determined to help him and sent him a financial gift, even though it meant sending it all the way to Rome. And that took more than a little doing in the first century. They did it to reassure him that their care for him was as strong as it had ever been, even though they were hundreds of miles apart.

Paul was deeply moved and told them as far as God was concerned their gifts were like a "sweet smelling sacrifice" (see Philippians 4:18). I suppose if he were writing today, Paul would have compared their generosity to very expensive perfume.

We need to remember this: God is not simply generous, He loves cheerful givers, too. All of which makes me wonder what lasting impression I will leave on Him this week.

28

STANDING OUT

It could only happen in real life. No one would believe it if you made it up. But it really did happen – in Dublin of all places. A thief was apprehended because of his 'colourful' boxer shorts!

The twenty-four-year-old stole some cigarettes from a local shop, but unfortunately for him, his trousers fell down as he was being chased by two bread delivery men. The youngster, who was also wearing odd shoes at the time, was duly arrested after the two men gave the police their very helpful, if highly unusual, description of the man (who had also threatened to kill them).

And it got me thinking. What do I do that makes me stand out? How will I be remembered on a day-to-day basis? Will it be for an unkind word or an unhelpful comment? Will people think of me as someone who is preoccupied with his own needs, or as a friend who took the time to show them that he cares?

I am constantly reminded that there are millions of lonely people living all around us. Research commissioned for the BBC in 2008, for example, found that UK society has become a far lonelier one over the last 30 years, with the result that "neighbourhoods in every part of the UK have become more socially fragmented".

And this is important because a report in 2017 also suggested that loneliness can prove as harmful to health as smoking fifteen cigarettes a day. Given this, I reckon a friendly visit could prove more than an encouragement – it might add a couple of years to someone's life.

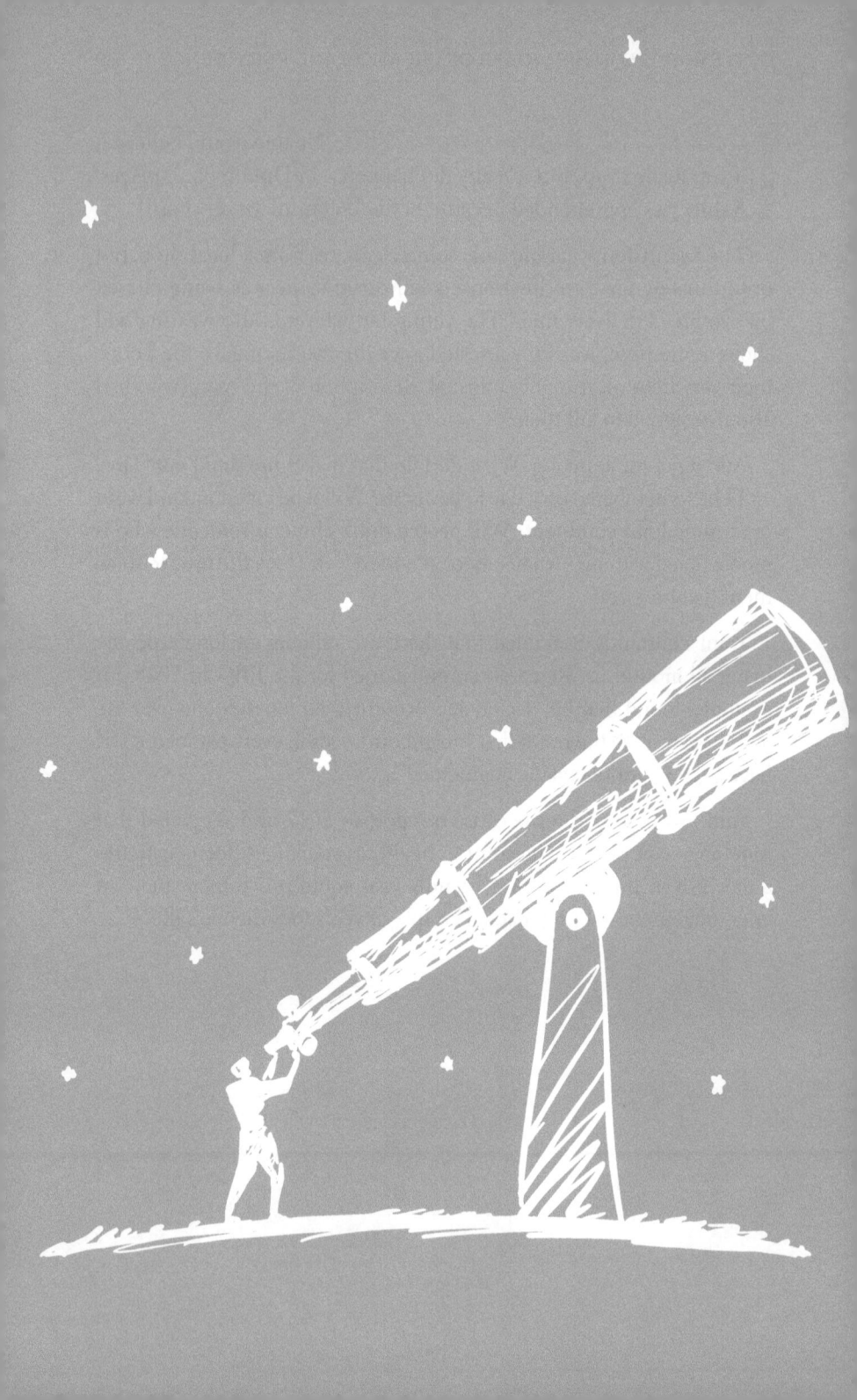

TRUST IN GOD

God will make that happen at the right time. He is the blessed and only Ruler, the King of all kings and the Lord of all lords. He is the only One who never dies.

He lives in light so bright no one can go near it. No one has ever seen God, or can see him. May honour and power belong to God forever. Amen.

1 Timothy 6:15-16.

29

MISTAKEN FOR JESUS

We have four fantastic boys, and God gave us an extra special treat by blessing us with twins. And what an amazing experience having twins has been. I often say it's been twice the work but ten times the fun, especially when people have not been able to tell the difference between them.

I particularly remember the hot summer day when the first of the twins got married. The photographic session seemed particularly long and tiring, which prompted the groom to ask his brother to take his place for a few minutes. Incredibly, only the bride seemed to notice the change, and she was used to their pranks by then.

Jesus was the perfect human being. He shows us what we should be like, indeed can be like, when we let Him take control of our lives. And as we know, He lived a life of compassionate love. He was in the business of offering forgiveness and hope and never looked for adulation because He wanted to serve others.

I wonder how much we look like Jesus. This world would be a far happier place if we spent a little more time wondering what we could do for others rather than for ourselves. As a colleague of mine said recently, "Let's unite to build a future that honours God. Let's unite around a vision of the world that is full of compassion, hope, integrity, understanding and where people listen to one another in deep respect, particularly and especially when we disagree. Let us live with selfless regard to the needs of others. For when all care, everyone is cared for."

30

STUPID IS AS STUPID DOES

Now I've asked some pretty stupid questions in my time, but few as crazy as the one I was asked a little while ago when I was sitting drinking a cup of coffee while admiring the stunning beauty of Pembrokeshire's Freshwater West.

I love 'Fresh West' and never cease to be entranced by its majestic beach. Anyone who has been there would know it only takes a moment or two after you step out of the car to reach the sand. And yet, to my amazement, on that warm Saturday morning, a car pulled up, and the driver shouted out of the passenger window, "Hey, mate. Can you tell me where I can find the beach?"

I thought he had to be kidding. If he had reached out, he could have almost touched the sand. But he wasn't. And I didn't imagine it, either, because several people around me also heard him say it. And so, I found myself smiling as I replied, "If you wind the driver's window down, you just might see it." He did, before driving off with a huge grin and a big wave.

Later that day, I was speaking to a group of Christians, and I used that story to remind them that God is always close to us, even though we can't see Him or may forget that He is present. Little did I know that the same young man was in the congregation!

"Well," I said when he introduced himself to me, "at least you'll know where the beach is next time." His reply left me speechless, "Oh, don't worry," he said. "I've been there before."

Ah well, I guess we can all do some daft things. I just hope we never forget that God is always close to us. In fact, He is only a prayer away.

31

THE STILL CENTRE OF THE STORM

I have no personal links with Haiti, but that doesn't mean I was unaffected by the plight of those who had to endure the lethal cocktail of wind and rain that came to be known as 'Hurricane Matthew'. And I was delighted to see the way so many ordinary people responded to their cries for help because I am sure of one thing: every act of kindness, no matter how small, brings a smile to God's face.

But the Christian faith is not just about doing good things. First and foremost, it is all about trust, and I was faced with a perfect example of this when my good friend Linda wrote to me as Hurricane Matthew bore down on her home in Daytona Beach, Florida.

"I slept very well last night and have chosen not to sit in front of the telly and be frightened and overwhelmed," she wrote. "I am in God's hands ... He knows my steps, and He has plans for me. I'm waiting for my orders from my King."

People often claim the Christian faith is irrelevant, or at best, little more than a crutch. I beg to differ. Perhaps you can see why, given the courage of people like Linda. And she is but one of the many believers I have seen trusting God when the storms are raging and the future looks bleak. In so doing, they discovered that He truly is a refuge and strength and always ready to help in times of trouble.

32

TRUSTWORTHY WOMEN

I am no sexist. I owe my life to a woman (my mother), and so I have no difficulty in affirming that behind every great man there must be a great woman (although Maryon Pearson's version is better – she reckons that behind every great man there is a surprised woman!). But it would now seem that behind many a living man there could be a woman doctor because researchers at Harvard have concluded that the sex of the doctor can have an influence on the number of patients who die. Indeed, they have calculated that approximately 32,000 lives a year would be saved in the US if male doctors behaved more like their female counterparts.

It is suggested that female doctors keep more patients alive because of the way they respond to the evidence. Now that's an amazing conclusion given the fact that men have often thought as first-century Judaism did. The ancient historian Josephus tells us that, in his day, women could not be called as witnesses "because of the levity and impetuosity of their sex". This, of course, is but a version of the common ancient (and not so ancient) prejudice that women are more easily swayed by their emotions and are therefore all-too-ready to jump to irrational conclusions.

And this reminded me that the very first witnesses to the resurrection of Jesus were women. And, in spite of the disparaging culture of their day, the first Christians were quite willing to say so, unapologetically. In doing so, they have provided us with a very powerful reason for trusting their claim that Jesus did rise from the dead. For no one would have been stupid enough to say that women were key witnesses unless it was the truth.

33

WAR AND PEACE

Most people today would associate the Roman Emperor Caesar Augustus with a census, a census that prompted Mary and Joseph to make their way to the ancient town of Bethlehem where she gave birth to the baby we know as Jesus. All of which is amazing given the fact that this had been predicted hundreds of years earlier!

I find it just as intriguing to reflect on the fact that at the very time the 'Prince of Peace' was being born in Judea, Augustus was building a temple to the god of war in Rome. Augustus was the undisputed leader of the Roman Empire and had embarked on an ambitious building programme to consolidate his victory in the most demonstrable way possible. His temple dedicated to Mars the Avenger was central to this.

I can't think of a better way of highlighting the nature of the message Jesus shared with His contemporaries and would also have us share with our world today. His values stand in stark contrast to so much of what we see going on around us. For Jesus expects us to forgive one another. He wants us to love each other. He will never force anyone to acknowledge Him as Lord, for He only wants those who are willing to put their trust in Him.

I chose to do that (eventually) because I became convinced that His way is the right way to live. And I did so in the knowledge that I have history on my side because even death was no match for Him.

34

GREAT EXPECTATIONS

A very good friend of mine told me a fascinating story about the distinguished psychologist Robert Rosenthal who taught his students a valuable lesson about the importance of expectation.

Rosenthal gave each of his students a rat and told them they had to train it to navigate a maze. Now, half of the class were told that they could expect poor results because their rats were genetically inferior, whereas the others were informed that theirs were of a much higher quality and so they could expect much more of them.

And sure enough, the results were exactly as Rosenthal predicted. Those he had said were 'good' performed much better than those he had described as 'poor'. But then, to everyone's surprise, Rosenthal revealed that the results had nothing to do with the rats.

The difference, he explained, was not in the rats but in the expectations of those who were dealing with them. Those who expected great things gave them their time and their energy, whereas the others expended very little effort on their rats because they saw little point in training them.

There's a valuable lesson there for us. If we expect little, we will probably achieve little, especially when it comes to dealing with people. And it's no different when it comes to God. If we expect little, we will give Him little time and attention. But those who expect great things from Him constantly discover that He is able to do infinitely more than we often think possible.

35

BREAKING THE SPELL

have to come clean. I have never been a *Harry Potter* fan, which clearly puts me in the minority given J. K. Rowling's popularity (by 2013, she had sold more than 500 million books). Whatever I think about her plots and storylines, though, she has clearly touched a nerve.

Sir Roger Scruton highlighted this in *A Point of View* on BBC Radio 4 and pointed to the fact that in Potter's world, human beings possess the power to change things at will as long as they have the proper spell. On the other hand, he suggested that 'religion' functions rather differently, for it expresses a sense of dependence – Christians pray but can't command (sadly, some Christians tend to see prayer as the latter because they seem convinced that God will always do what they ask Him to do). But prayer, as Scruton rightly understands, should always reveal our dependence on God. We should come to Him knowing that He can do the seemingly impossible but recognising that He is not at our beck and call.

Prayer, then, is really an expression of our trust. We can – and should – bring everything to God in prayer, all the while understanding that He always knows what is best for us. And that certainly doesn't mean we'll enjoy a carefree life. Jesus clearly didn't, so why should we expect anything different?

36

SHINING LIGHTS, NOT SHADY CHARACTERS

was reminded of the philosopher Diogenes recently. Lots of people nowadays will *not* have heard of this quirky character, but that was far from the case in the fourth century BC.

Diogenes was controversial and must have been very difficult to live with. He used his simple lifestyle (he begged for a living and often slept in a large ceramic jar in the marketplace, for example) to criticise what he saw as the corrupt and confused values of the society in which he lived.

He was not easily intimidated by the 'great and the good', either. It's said that when his famous contemporary Alexander the Great asked him if he could do anything to help him, he simply told him to get out of the way because he was hiding the sun.

I have been somewhat 'haunted' by that phrase because it reminded me of how easily I can hide the light that comes from a very different sun – the 'Son' of God.

It seems to me that every time I fail to forgive someone, every time I am tempted to be selfish rather than generous and every time I am puffed up by my own sense of self-importance, I make it more difficult for people to see the Jesus I claim to follow. There are lots of other ways I can do that, of course, but when it comes down to it, I've come to the conclusion that I need to remind myself on a daily basis that it's a cop-out to ask people to look at Jesus but ignore the church. He expects Christians to be the light of the world rather than the reason for an eclipse of the Son!

37

A DOUBTFUL GENIUS

The film was good, but the book is much, much better. I'm talking about *The Enigma*, which tells the fascinating story of Alan Turing "whose cipher-cracking transformed the Second World War". Turing was an incredible mathematician and is credited with being the father of theoretical computer science and artificial intelligence. It's even been suggested that his pivotal role at Bletchley Park (Britain's wartime code-breaking centre) could have helped shorten the war by as much as two years and saved as many as fourteen million lives.

Turing was a remarkable, in fact, remarkably complex character, whose behaviour seemed to create challenges for so many of those who had to engage with him. I was particularly struck by the way he was quite willing to doubt the wisdom of his day, even when others found his attitude more than a little difficult.

I suppose I warmed to Turing's approach because this is how I came to faith. People often make the mistake of thinking that doubt and faith are mutually exclusive. But they are not. Faith implies trust rather than certainty. And thankfully, that is all that God asks of us in this life.

I came to faith kicking and screaming, but I ended up believing when I discovered that the evidence is very convincing. I have not regretted it, either, because God has enriched my life in so many wonderful ways. And, just as importantly, He has assured me that the best is yet to be.

It's why I enjoy the Advent season so much. It's an annual reminder of what I can look forward to when Jesus comes back.

38

WHEN LIFE DOESN'T MAKE SENSE

She may be a lot older than me, but she's still amazingly sharp, and she possesses a lovely sense of humour.

"Have you heard about the chap who had a chat with his creator?" she asked me.

"No, I haven't," I replied. "Tell me about him."

"Well," she went on, "he wanted to know what a million years meant to God. To which God replied, 'A mere second.' 'And what about a million pounds?' he continued. 'Oh, that's a mere penny!' God said. 'In which case,' the man replied, 'could you give me a million pounds?' But as you would expect, God came back with the perfect response: 'Hang on a second!'"

I had to laugh. It was much, much better than the jokes I usually tell. But I am well aware that for many of us, life is often far from funny. Sad things do happen, and we often don't or can't understand why God allows it. As someone once said, there are times when God simply doesn't seem to make sense.

It's at moments like these that we all have to make a choice: will we trust Him or not? Jesus chose to trust His Heavenly Father even as He was being crucified. And down through the centuries, countless others have decided to do the same, too. William Cowper was one of these, which is why He was able to write this hymn:

God moves in a mysterious way, His wonders to perform;
He plants His footsteps in the sea and rides upon the storm.

Deep in unfathomable mines of never-failing skill
He treasures up His bright designs and works His sov'reign will.

Ye fearful saints, fresh courage take; the clouds ye so much dread
Are big with mercy and shall break in blessings on your head.

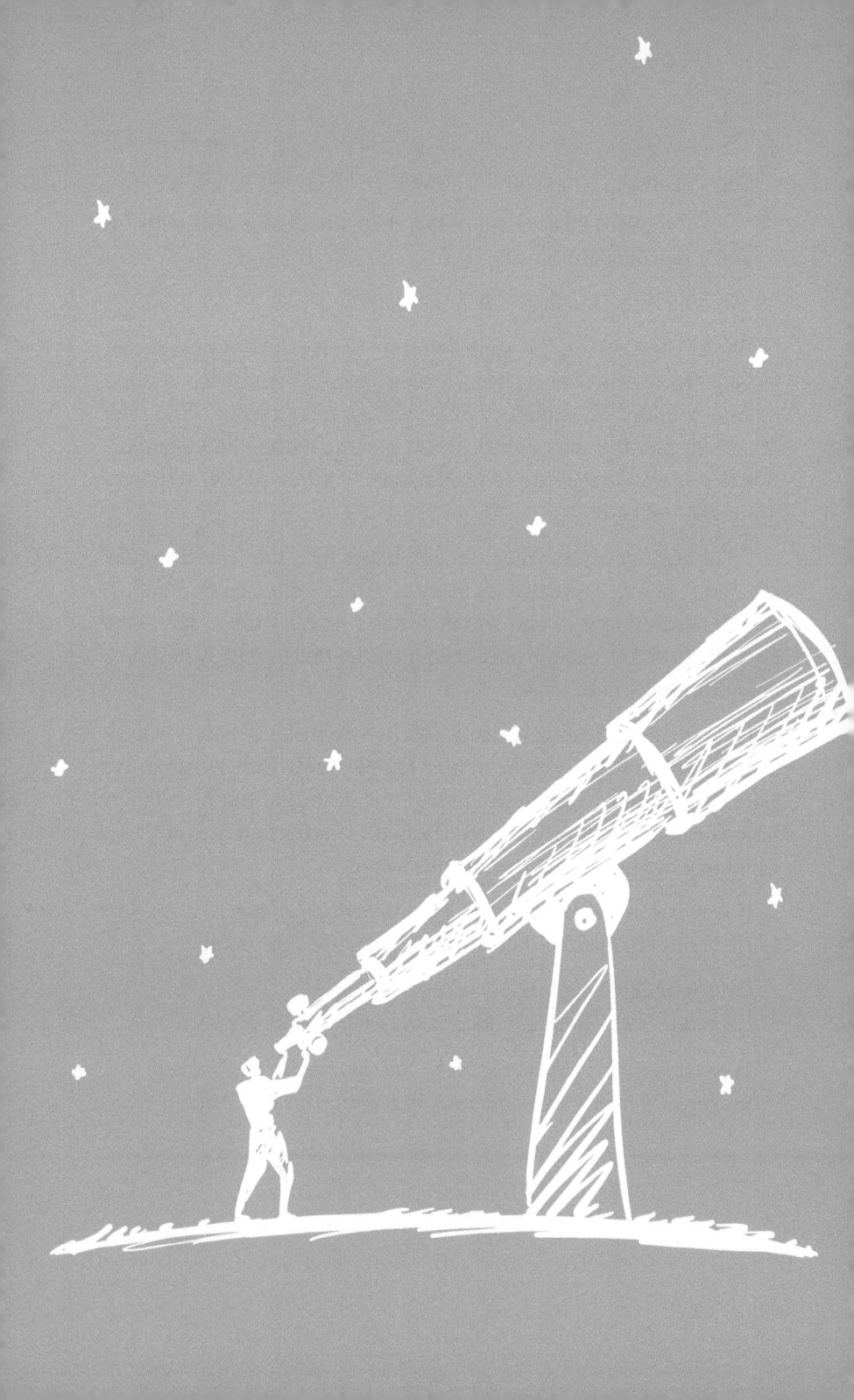

POWER OF GOD

*Jesus looked at them and said,
"For people this is impossible, but for God
all things are possible."*

Matthew 19:26.

39

THE BUTTERFLY EFFECT

My wife and I met Jill in Turkey about twenty years ago, and she had a very sad tale to tell. Her husband had died very suddenly when they were holidaying in France a year or two before, and this had left her bewildered and bereft, not least because he had planned to become a missionary.

But far from being depressed, Jill was full of faith and hope, and I realised why when she told me her story, a story she repeated on the TV show *Songs of Praise* a few weeks later. It seems that she had been sitting beside his grave sometime after his death, pondering her future and despairing of her loss, when she saw two things in immediate succession.

The first was a rainbow, and this reminded her of the Old Testament story of Noah's ark, which reassured her that God always keeps a promise. And then, to her absolute amazement, she saw a chrysalis transform into a butterfly before her very eyes.

And this rekindled her hope because she recalled the biblical promise: *We shall not all sleep, but we shall all be changed, in a moment, in the twinkling of an eye, at the last trumpet.* (1 Corinthians 15:51-51, ESV).

Jill's story reminded me that, ultimately, this is what Christianity is all about: resurrection. As former bishop N. T. Wright has often said, Christians don't simply believe in life after death, they believe in life after life after death.

40

A GUIDING HAND

The Jews, wrote Jonathon Sacks, had a history longer and more remarkable than most. They were the first to find God in history and understand it as a coherent narrative, rather than just a random sequence of events. But for all that, he says, classical Hebrew had no word for 'history' because Judaism organised itself around the concept of memory rather than history; what happened to their ancestors had formed part of their experience and was their life-story, too. In other words, it was 'family history'.

We should never forget the terrible cost of war, whether on nations or on particular individual lives. War can have a devastating effect on those involved and can do more than destroy people's mental equilibrium and sense of well-being. It can also destroy their faith in God. Wilfred Owen hinted at this when he wrote his fantastic poem *Futility*. Gazing at a dead young soldier, he wrote:

O what made fatuous sunbeams toil
To break earth's sleep at all?

In stark contrast to Owen, the author of Psalm 46 assures us that *God is our refuge and strength, always ready to help in times of trouble.* (verse 1, NLT). And it's worth remembering that the psalmist wrote these words because he had seen God helping his people in a time of national emergency, and it gave him a sense of hope in the face of everything else happening to him and his people.

Winston Churchill said something similar in 1942. "I sometimes have a feeling of interference, I want to stress that," he said. "I have a feeling sometimes that some Guiding Hand has interfered. I have a feeling that we have a Guardian because we have a great cause." And then he said, "And we shall have that Guardian as long as we serve that cause faithfully." Now there's a challenge.

41

A BIT OF A BLOOMER

I've made lots of mistakes over the years, but none as catastrophic as the one I came across the other day when I discovered that a "Mrs Bloom of Minnesota" had telephoned her husband because she was experiencing problems with the central heating. The results were nothing short of disastrous.

Mrs Bloom was feeling cold and had failed to get her boiler working properly, and so, as a first step, her son told her to set the thermostat a little higher. No big shakes, you would think, but unfortunately, she thought he had said, "Set the thermostat on fire." Which she duly did – with the help of a blow torch! Thankfully, Mrs Bloom managed to escape with her life, but tragically, the resulting fire destroyed her home.

We all make mistakes, of course, and few have such calamitous consequences, thankfully. Mrs Bloom's sad story is a salutary reminder that we need to listen carefully, particularly when we are asking for advice.

And this is no truer than when it comes to the issue of death, which is why we would all do well to listen to these wonderful words of Jesus. *"Do not let your hearts be troubled,"* He said. *"Trust in God, trust also in me. In my Father's house are many rooms. I am going to prepare a place for you."* (see John 14:1-2). Now that's clear enough. Put simply, Jesus has told us that if we place our trust in Him, our eternal futures are safe in His hands.

42

THE MOST IMPORTANT QUESTION IN LIFE

've never been one for Halloween. I don't find it helpful to focus on the dark side of life. In 2017, I had the perfect excuse, because October 31st marked the 500th anniversary of the day when a deeply troubled (and troublesome) monk named Martin Luther nailed his 95 *Theses* to the door of Wittenberg Castle Church. He did it in defiance of papal authority, and in so doing, unleashed a torrent of theological and political debate that eventually ripped the church and Western Europe asunder.

Much has already been said about Luther's actions, and I am sure much more will be said in the days and years to come, both in praise and in criticism of this seismic moment. As one of my Baptist colleagues wrote, "We should thank God for the Reformation and praise God for the Reformers – but we should acknowledge where they went wrong, too."

I have highlighted the Reformation for one very important reason: the real bone of contention is as valid and as disturbing today as it was then. It demands an answer to a very simple but equally important question: how do you recognise the true people of God?

The first Christians claimed that this had nothing to do with gender or ethnicity, quality of lifestyle or religious devotion. It's all down to our willingness to let Jesus be the Lord of our lives. A Jewish Pharisee named Saul of Tarsus finally did it. The German monk Martin Luther eventually understood it. And this former atheist became convinced of it. And so it will continue, because some things, like the English rain, never change.

43

A REMARKABLE RESEMBLANCE

I don't watch the *Graham Norton Show* very often, but I'm glad I did when he held a fascinating interview with British movie star Gary Oldman. And it convinced me to make the effort to see him playing Winston Churchill in Joe Wright's *Darkest Hour*.

I was particularly struck by what he had to say about the way they worked on his appearance so that he ended up looking uncannily like Churchill. In fact, it's nothing short of miraculous.

It seems that Oldman had been told he faced the prospect of putting on 50-60 pounds in weight if he wanted to play the part, but quite sensibly, he concluded that this would prove ridiculously unhealthy. And so, he opted for the easier option: he persuaded makeup artist Kazuhiro Tsuji to come out of retirement just to work on the film. And the results are simply staggering.

When I look at Jesus, I see what I am supposed to be like, not least in my willingness to trust God whatever the circumstances and to go around doing good wherever and whenever I can. And, thankfully, that's not unachievable, because clever as Kazuhiro Tsuji is, he is no match for the God who can make me more and more like His Son. It's no easy process, of course. It takes time and effort. But it was no different for Oldman, for he had to endure up to four hours a day in a makeup chair! But to become more and more like Jesus? That's got to be worth the effort, surely?

44

A JOLLY SAILOR

I reckon you have to be rather special to have someone like Falklands War hero Simon Weston describe you as an "incredible man". But that was his response to the death of Cornish-born surgeon Captain Rick Jolly. Known as "Doc", Jolly was the senior medical officer of Plymouth-based 3 Commando Brigade and ran the field hospital at Ajax Bay where about 1,000 troops were treated. "Without his organisational skills, the surgeons and medics would never have functioned," Weston said. "I can only thank him for saving my life, and many others." In fact, the records show that, even though he had to work in the most awful of conditions, Doc saved the life of every British serviceman he treated. A remarkable achievement indeed!

But even more remarkably, Captain Jolly OBE was also awarded the Orden de Mayo (Order of May) by the Argentinean government for the way he treated their injured servicemen. I find that truly inspirational because it reminds me of something Jesus said in the Sermon on the Mount. Let me remind you:

"You have heard the law that says, 'Love your neighbour' and hate your enemy. But I say, love your enemies! Pray for those who persecute you! In that way, you will be acting as true children of your Father in heaven. For he gives his sunlight to both the evil and the good, and he sends rain on the just and the unjust alike. If you love only those who love you, what reward is there for that? Even corrupt tax collectors do that much. If you are kind only to your friends, how are you different from anyone else? Even pagans do that. But you are to be perfect, even as your Father in heaven is perfect." (Matthew 5:43-48, NLT).

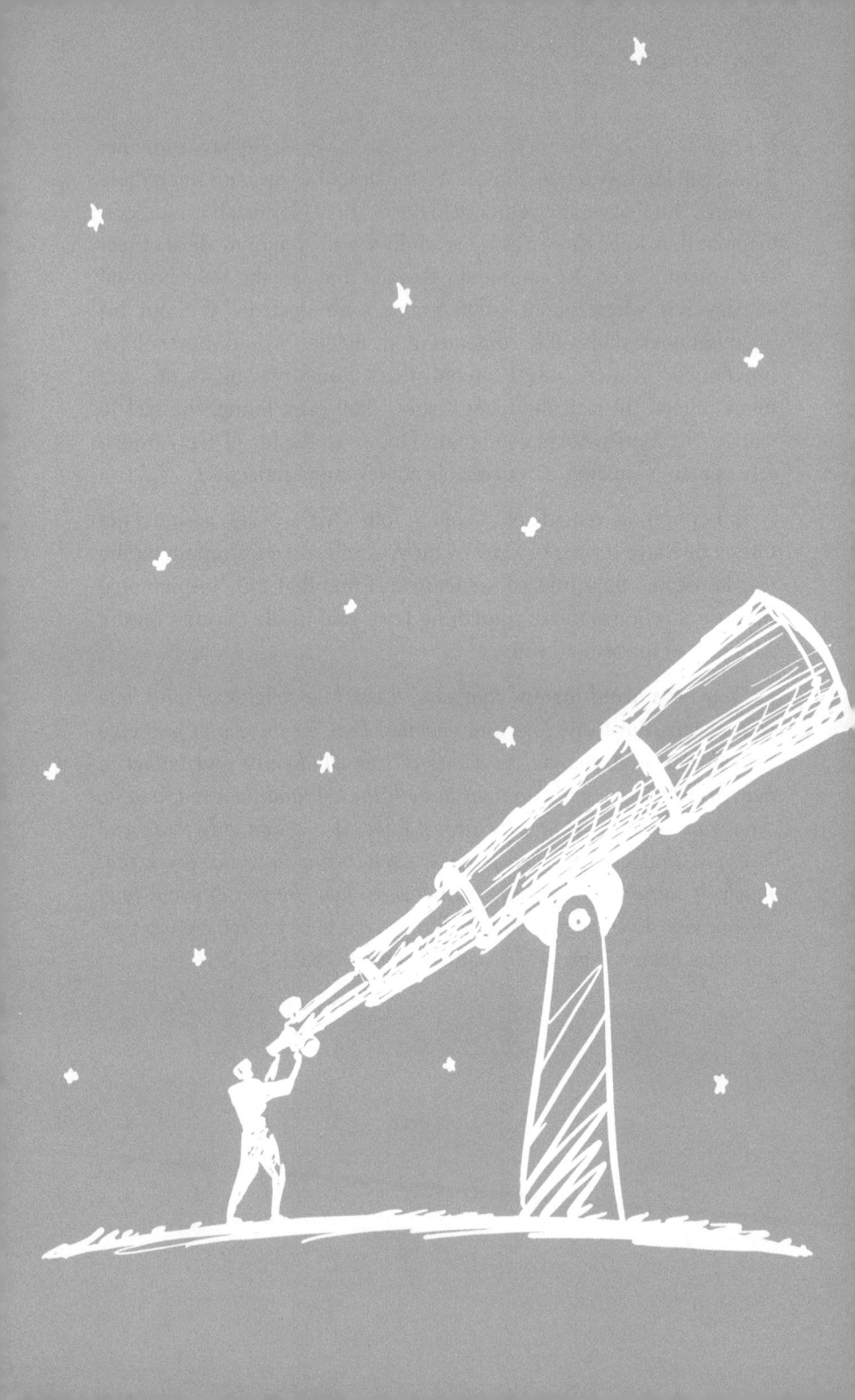

NOTHING TOO DIFFICULT FOR GOD

*"I am the Lord,
the God of every person on the earth.
Nothing is impossible for me."*
Jeremiah 32:27.

45

WILFULLY DEAF

I will never forget the morning I met Mike and Mary (not their real names) to plan their wedding. It was a very happy occasion. They were both widowed, and life had been tough for both of them in recent years. But, to everyone's delight, they had found a new sense of happiness and purpose in each other's love.

Now, as we all know, marriage can prove highly challenging, even for those with experience and a sense of humour. The divorce statistics underline this truth all too clearly. And so, in spite of their age and previous track records, I suggested it would be good to spend a little time together reflecting on their hopes and dreams for the future.

But Mike was adamant: he did not want marriage counselling. As far as he was concerned, he had no need of it. And much as I tried to change his resolve, I failed. And so, I finally said, "But Mike, what makes you so sure you don't need counselling?" "Ah, Rob," he replied pointing to his hearing aid. "It's quite simple. I can always switch it off!"

He was joking, of course – at least, I think he was! But if you stop and think about it for a moment, Mike was merely highlighting a common human weakness. We often refuse to listen to things that challenge us. I see this happening quite regularly, not least when I try to tell people what Jesus can do for them. I hope I never get to the point where I refuse to listen to things that might unsettle me.

46

FORGIVE US OUR DEBTS

It's staggering to think that the level of unsecured debt is now reckoned to average £13,000 per household. Now, I'm no financial whiz kid; in fact, I constantly give thanks that I have a wife who can keep our house in order.

But even I find this level of debt unnerving, and it makes me increasingly determined to support the work of *Christians Against Poverty*. CAP is an incredibly effective debt counselling charity. And its services are free. It makes my day every time I'm told that yet another person is now debt free.

Now, interestingly enough, this is the kind of imagery the Bible uses when it talks of our sin. "Forgive us our trespasses," we pray as we are reminded that God expects us to do the same.

I'm often told that Christianity is not just boring, but it's completely irrelevant, too. People who think like that need to talk to the man I baptised who told me he can now sleep at night because of what his faith has done for him. Alternatively, they would do well to chat with the young mother I met some years ago. She was wracked with guilt because of something she had done in the past. But when we prayed together, she said she saw a snow-covered field, and it reminded her of a promise that God made more than 2,000 years ago: *"though your sins are like scarlet, they shall be as white as snow."* (Isaiah 1:8, ESV). Irrelevant? Anything but. It's why Christianity is such good news.

47

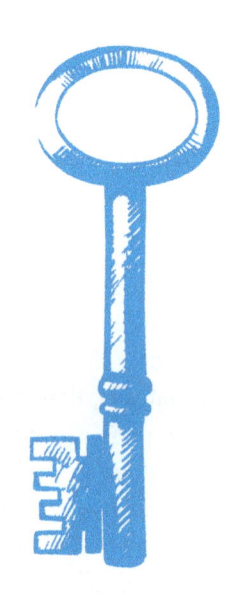

THE KEY TO SUCCESS

I've met some amazing people in my time, and they have taught me so much about God. Take Malcolm. Following his discharge from the army, Malcolm became a chronic alcoholic and then a petty criminal. And, as a result, was finally sent to prison. If you'd known Malcolm then, you would have said that his future was anything but rosy. But God had other ideas, and so He arranged for him to meet the local vicar. And he told him that God could do more than help him with his addiction, he promised him that God could give him a completely new life – and all for free.

Malcolm was no fool. He knew a good deal when he saw one, so he asked God to forgive him and to help him change his lifestyle. And that's exactly what God did because Malcolm finally became a probation officer. In fact, as I understand it, Malcolm was the first criminal ever accepted by the Home Office for training. And Malcolm discovered that God has a sense of humour, too, because his first posting was to the prison where he'd served as a prisoner. And as you might guess, the wardens found it very difficult indeed to give him a set of keys to the prison. But that's what God is like. He can take any life and change it for the better. After all, He is in the restoration business.

48

FOOD FOR THOUGHT

You don't have to live very long to appreciate that people can be very fickle. If you want a good example of this, just think of what happened after Jesus fed a congregation of 5,000 people when all He had to hand was a small packed lunch.

The crowds got so excited that they tried to make Him their king. They were convinced that if He could perform miracles like that, He could do anything, even lead a successful revolt against Rome.

But Jesus was having none of it. He had no intention of using violence or fermenting a political revolution. His approach stands in stark contrast to the embittered, twisted logic of the terrorist, and for that matter, much of church history, too. For His was a revolution of love, a love so revolutionary that it even encompassed His enemies.

But Jesus knew that His message would be hard to digest. He was sure it would prove very unpopular, not least because of the emphasis He placed on our spiritual needs. In fact, the Galilean crowds left in droves, and He was left with a tiny group of devoted, if very imperfect, disciples. They decided to 'hang on in there' because they concluded He had the answers to the really important questions in life.

So, what's new? People still reject His message in large numbers, but I never lose heart, because I know there will always be those who choose to follow Him. And for one very simple reason: He offers us life with a capital 'L'.

49

FEARFULLY AND WONDERFULLY MADE

I reckon few, if any, of us, have not been affected by the agonising tale of young Charlie Gard, the eleven-month-old baby boy who finally died in July 2017 after a desperately tragic battle against a rare form of mitochondrial disease. Who would have guessed that just a year earlier such a small bundle of joy would have such a worldwide impact, prompting messages from the Pope and President Trump as well as death threats against medical staff at Great Ormond Street Hospital?

So, what can we learn from it all? Lots of things, I guess, but the one thing that stood out for me is the way in which people everywhere appreciated the significance of one human life. And that's something worth treasuring given the way we tend to treat one another on a regular basis. Human nature being what it is, we can devalue one another and take each other for granted, as well as stab one another in the front and back, both metaphorically, as well as physically.

Charlie Gard's short life is a tragic but very powerful reminder that we are all very special and deserve to be treasured because we have been created in the image of God Himself. And I'm sure of one thing: this world would be a much better place if we reminded ourselves of that simple truth when we got out of bed in the morning.

50

CONFIDENT FAITH

It was like déjà vu. I was travelling back from a preaching engagement in November 2017 when my son telephoned and asked if we had heard the news from Texas. We hadn't, but when he told us about the shootings that had taken place at Sutherland Springs Baptist Church, it reminded me of the day that a lone gunman entered a church in Fort Worth, Texas, some eighteen years before, killing seven people before finally shooting himself.

I remember watching TV footage at the time, but I can identify with what happened much more now because I have since come to know the pastor and others who were there at the time.

The story of what took place at Wedgewood Baptist Church on that dreadful night in 1999 is both sobering and encouraging. It is a helpful reminder of how wicked human beings can be, but it's also become a huge encouragement to my faith.

Few will ever have heard of Jeremiah Neitz, but he was the young man who stood up and told the killer to shoot him because he knew where he would go if he did! And it prompted Larry Gene Ashbrook to turn the gun on himself. Given this act of courage, who could ever say, "You have to be a wimp to be a Christian"? Even more importantly, given this kind of down-to-earth faith, who would dare to say it's irrelevant?

51

IT'S NOT FAIR

love a nice 'murder mystery', and in my opinion, no one does it better than Agatha Christie. And so, I took very little persuading to pop along to the Torch Theatre in Milford to wallow in Kenneth Branagh's highly successful adaptation of *Murder on the Orient Express*.

I loved it, even though I have to admit that Branagh never had a chance when it came to playing Hercule Poirot. As far as I'm concerned, David Suchet will always be the definitive Belgian with the "little grey cells".

When I got back home, I found myself reflecting on Poirot's final comments and the conclusions he had drawn from this particular murder. As far as he was concerned, there was no justice to be found in the case.

Lots of people seem to feel like this. It begins early in life, too. "It's not fair," seems to come naturally to every one of us, even in the school playground.

So where does this instinct come from and why should we believe it matters? I reckon atheists struggle to answer questions like this, whereas I have a very simple response. We are all created in the image of a God who is completely committed to justice, and our innate desire for it is a reminder of that wonderful truth. The Anglican scholar Tom Wright put it much more eloquently than me when he said, "…this longing for things to be put right, remains one of the great human goals and dreams. Christians believe this is so because all humans have heard, deep within themselves, the echo of a voice which calls us to live like that."

52

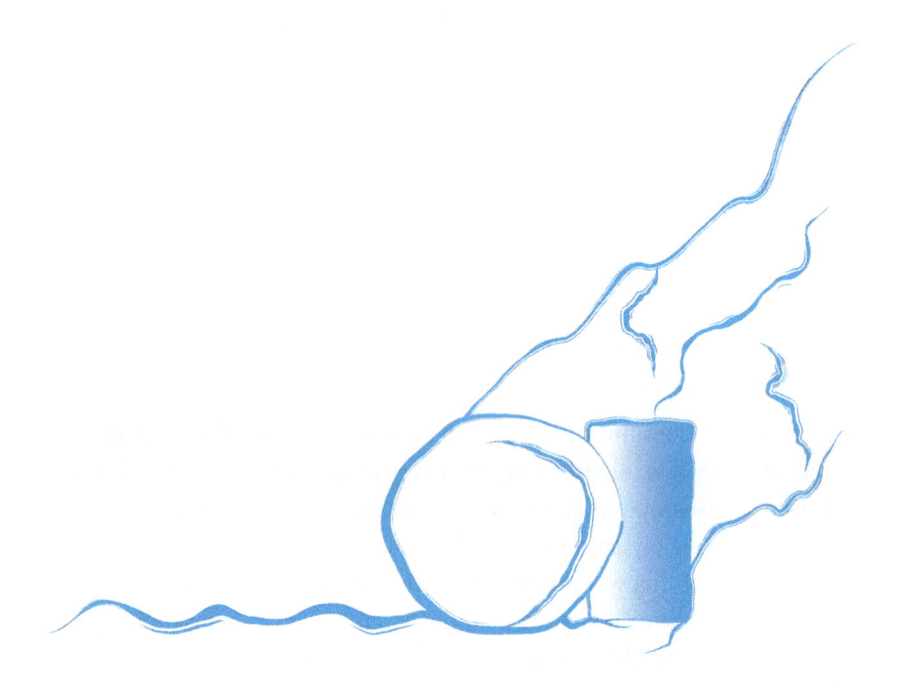

EMPTY PROOF

I have met some fascinating people in my time, not least when I was invited to lead tours for a Christian holiday company. I especially remember Mike (not his real name) because he had a very unusual story to tell.

Mike was a high-ranking officer in the British army, and when we met, he was a converted Christian, who was fully persuaded about the reality of Jesus. But this had not always been the case. In fact, there had been a time when he had no interest in God whatsoever. But things changed dramatically the day he visited Jerusalem and wandered into what he later discovered was The Garden Tomb. As he arrived, a stranger approached him and told him he was expecting him. "Follow me," he said, and without thinking, Mike did.

The stranger stopped outside the tomb and asked Mike to look inside. As Mike did, the stranger asked, "So what do you see?"

"Nothing," Mike replied. "It's empty."

"That's right. You're absolutely correct," the stranger replied. "Now explain it," he said and promptly walked away.

Mike never did discover the identity of the stranger, but he did come up with an answer to the question. He came to the conclusion that the tomb was empty because Jesus had risen from the dead, and this persuaded him to become a Christian.

I can readily identify with Mike. I came to the same conclusion when I was teaching History in the early 1970s. And I still reckon it makes the most sense of the evidence. What about you?

REFERENCES

The author wishes to acknowledge the sources of the quotes used and the stories referred to in this book.

Thought 2	Taylor, R. (2016) 'How long should you wash your hands for? One verse of God Save The Queen! Medical chief says proper cleaning takes 45 seconds', *Mail Online*, 18 November. Available at: https://www.dailymail.co.uk/news/article-3948130/How-long-wash-hands-One-verse-God-Save-Queen-Medical-chief-says-proper-cleaning-takes-45-seconds.html [accessed November 2018]
	McMillen, S. I. (1984) *None Of These Diseases*. UK. Marshall, Morgan and Scott. p. 25.
Thought 4	Misselbrook, L. and Misselbrook, M. (1987) *Love Won Another*. UK. Marshall, Morgan and Scott. p.122-123.
Thought 7	Thomas, E. (2000) 'Bobby at the Brink', *Newsweek* (online), 13 August. Available at: https://www.newsweek.com/bobby-brink-159013 [accessed November 2018]

REFERENCES

Thought 9	Travis, S. H. (1982) *I believe in the Second Coming of Jesus*. London. Hodder and Stoughton. p. 235.
Thought 14	Buckeridge, J. (1999) *100 Instant Discussion Starters*. Eastbourne. Kingsway. p.180.
Thought 17	Clements, R. (1986) *Introducing Jesus*. Eastbourne. Kingsway. p.53.
Thought 20	Buckeridge, J. (1999) *100 Instant Discussion Starters*. Eastbourne. Kingsway. p.83.
Thought 28	Ferguson, F. (2018) 'Knife robber caught thanks to description of 'colourful' boxer shorts after his trousers fell down while escaping', *Independent.ie* (online), 15 February. Available at: https://www.independent.ie/irish-news/courts/knife-robber-caught-thanks-to-description-of-colourful-boxer-shorts-after-his-trousers-fell-down-while-escaping-36608291.html [accessed November 2018]
	Easton, M. (2008) 'Life in UK 'has become lonelier'', *BBC News* (online), 1 December. Available at: http://news.bbc.co.uk/1/hi/uk/7755641.stm [accessed November 2018]
	Unnamed Journalist (2018) 'Minister for loneliness appointed to continue Jo Cox's work', *BBC News* (online), 17 January. Available at: https://www.bbc.co.uk/news/uk-42708507 [accessed November 2018]
Thought 32	Maryon Pearson (2018) *Wikipedia*. Available at: https://en.wikipedia.org/wiki/Maryon_Pearson [accessed November 2018]

Parker-Pope, T. (2018) 'Should You Choose a Female Doctor?', *The New York Times* (online), 14 August. Available at: https://www.nytimes.com/2018/08/14/well/doctors-male-female-women-men-heart.html [accessed November 2018]

Bauckham, R. *The Women at the Tomb: The Credibility of their Story* (pdf). p.4. Available at: http://richardbauckham.co.uk/uploads/Accessible/The%20Women%20&%20the%20Resurrection.pdf [accessed November 2018]

Thought 34 Misselbrook, L. and Misselbrook, M. (1987) *Love Won Another*. UK. Marshall, Morgan and Scott. p.17.

Thought 35 BBC Radio 4 (2017) 'Pottering towards the new socialist state', *A point of View*, 27 August. Available at: https://www.bbc.co.uk/programmes/b091wf88 [accessed November 2018]

Thought 36 Diogenes the Cynic, translated by Hard, R. (2012) *Sayings and Anecdotes with Other Popular Moralists*. New York. Oxford University Press. p.xi.

Thought 37 Hodges, A. (2014) *Alan Turing: The Enigma. The Book that Inspired the Film The Imitation Game*. London. Vintage Books. Back cover.

Thought 38 Cowper, W. (1774) *God Moves in a Mysterious Way*. Public Domain. Available at: https://hymnary.org/text/god_moves_in_a_mysterious_way [accessed November 2018]

REFERENCES

Thought 39 — Wright, N. T. (2004) *Life After Life After Death: Resurrection of Jesus*. USA. Augsburg Fortress Publishing.

Thought 40 — Sacks, J. (2018) 'The Story We Tell (Ki Tavo 5778)', *The Office of Rabbi Sacks* (online blog), 28 August. Available at: http://rabbisacks.org/story-tell-ki-tavo-5778/ [accessed November 2018]

Edited by Roberts, M. and revised by Porter, P. (1982) *The Faber Book of Modern Verse*. London. Faber and Faber Limited. p.191.

Gardner, D. E. (1983) *The Trumpet Sounds for Britain, Vol. 2: Gods Great Miracles Of Deliverance*. Great Britain. Christian Foundations Publications. Cover note.

Thought 41 — Buckeridge, J. (1999) *100 Instant Discussion Starters*. Eastbourne. Kingsway. p.36.

Thought 43 — *The Graham Norton Show* (2017) BBC 1, 31 December.

Thought 44 — Unnamed Journalist (2018) 'Falklands War 'true hero' Captain Rick Jolly dies', *BBC News* (online), 15 January. Available at: https://www.bbc.co.uk/news/uk-england-cornwall-42682005 [accessed November 2018]

Thought 46 — Milligan, B. (2017) 'UK household debt now a record £13,000, says TUC', *BBC News* (online), 8 January. Available at: https://www.bbc.co.uk/news/business-38534238 [accessed November 2018]

Thought 51 | Wright, T. (2006) *Simply Christian*. London. SPCK Publishing. p.14.